The Woman EVERY Man Wants

Volume 1

Raheem Turane

A Woman EVERY Man Wants by Raheem Turane
Published by Raheem Turane Communications & Media Group, LLC

All rights reserved. No part of this publication may be reproduced, distributed, or transmitted in any form or by any means, including photocopying, recording, or other electronic or mechanical methods without written permission of the publisher, except in the case of brief quotations embodied in critical reviews and certain other noncommercial uses permitted by the United States of America copyright law.

Artwork by: Ni'cole Conaway
Cover design by: Couture Graphics

All scripture quotations, unless otherwise indicated, are taken from the King James Version (Authorized Version). First published in 1611.

Copyright © 2017 Raheem Turane
All rights reserved.
ISBN-10: 0692860975
ISBN-13: 978-0692860977

Dedication

This book is dedicated to everyone who reminded me that this is just a small thing in the BIG plans of God for my life.

Raheem Turane

Table of Contents

Dedication ………………………………………...i

Foreword ………………………………………… iii

Preface ………………………………………… xi

Introduction ………………………………………… xvii

Where to Place her Friends …………………………1

The value of Holding On ……………………………19

Wisdom and Discernment ………………………… 37

Who isn't Afraid of Work …………………………47

Isn't Afraid to Ask for what She Wants ……………71

Who will Listen and Accept Counsel ………………89

Thank You ……………………………………….....111

Booking …………………………………………..117

Coming Soon……………………………………..118

Foreword

"The Woman EVERY Man Wants"

It's a startling and frightening truth that some statistics show that 40% to 50% of marriages end in divorce due to various factors such as finances, age difference, infidelity and much more. It makes one wonder where does the "till death do us part" play in the decision making? What makes things get to the point that two people who vow to love each other get to a place where they can no longer stand being in the same house? These questions ring in many of our minds who have experienced divorce, especially those like myself who has been divorced twice. What is the problem? Is it me? The men? Society? Who is to blame for the failed covenant act that the Lord first set in motion in the Garden of Eden with Adam and Eve? For centuries, many have tried to come up with this answer through scientific studies, experiments, and counseling or through various books and paraphernalia, some helped and others did not. I was seeking a deeper answer, one that would lead me to a path making wiser and more thought-out decisions. It's painful to be in love with someone and then the relationship falls apart. It's like having a cupcake in your hand and when you try to take a bite it just crumbles into pieces. In my journey I realized the first step was starting with me, the inner me, the little girl that was now a full grown woman. A woman that had to make decisions, life changing ones.

    One of the reasons most relationships fail is because the person seeking the relationship has not found self-love in themselves. They are fragmented and looking for that one person to put the pieces together, not realizing they're supposed to be whole themselves. Then coming down the lane in my instance it was me doing this and I would connect with a man in the same situation, so now you have two broken people trying to put the other together.

My focus was no longer working on my inner battles, struggles, and issues but rather focusing on his and trying to fix them. He was doing the exact same thing on his side, yet this was not the answer. One cannot fix another broken person when they have not lived the life or felt the inner pain that cracked that person, they cannot forgive the transgressor that that person may need to confront, and they cannot give that self-confidence to a person who does not see it in themselves. They cannot erase the pain but only cover it. Now, two people are in a situation who do not have a clue of what the other person needs or what they are looking for themselves. These individuals only have the ability to fix what the natural eye sees based on their own hurtful experiences. What people really need to understand is simple, but complex. It's simple because we should know what the other person needs but it's complex because many of us don't know what we want or need. What is it that I must do or have to be complete within myself so I can connect and attract a man who is complete and knows what I need? It has to start with me, then my path will connect with the "he" that God has for me.

As I began to soul search while being prepared for my soul mate, I had to deal with my deep rooted issues, of pain, being abused, low self-esteem, disciplining my spending, and learning to build up a man up with my words instead of tearing him down. Sacrifices had to be met and they had to be met willingly by my submission to God and not forcefully by my future mate who had no clue I had issues. I had to forgive those whom I had soul ties with because I wanted to be pure in my heart for this special man whom God would send me. I wanted to bring him pure love with no hesitations and give him my whole heart with no reservations. I had to learn to hold his hand and be a part of his backbone when we would go through wars and trials the world would send our way. I had to learn how to understand his quietness when words couldn't be spoken. I had to learn how to be a woman that a Godly man wants.

This is why I was so excited to read the powerful words that Raheem Turane had written in "A Woman EVERY Man Wants." The title threw me, because I had seen a few books out about the topic but not one that touched me to the core as this one. As I read the words, I could feel the transparency coming from his heart as he shared his heart-wrenching testimony, identifying the areas that he had faulted in during his relationships within his family and his failed marriage. The pains of a man who had to reach deep into his soul to be a guide to help women as myself understand a man's point of view. It's also a testament to men that it's ok to be raw and transparent, it's strength to show your emotions and let women know you feel pain also. The words moved my heart yet the biblical verses expounded upon added a human side of this saga and gave it a powerful spiritual push. This was not just the words of a man writing a book but the Spirit of God confirming through his servant the truth of his testimony and God's design for man and woman. That alone lets us know that this is not just a natural thing but more spiritual than anything in the world. It's a covenant with the divine being and Raheem clearly connects them both with his testimony and God. Truly we see what a man wants and needs in a woman not based on his selfish needs but the need to keep the unity of the marriage in its original covenant state.

The clarity and wisdom in this book will have everyone doing self-evaluation. It's an easy read that will keep you flipping pages and soul searching as you turn each page absorbing each one like a sponge overflowing, pleading to be released. It makes you go back and meditate on things that you should've changed and still have time to change. It's as though by reading this book, Gods hand has reached out to us and said, "Child, you have a second chance at love. Let me show you a more excellent way." Truly I felt renewed, enlightened and refreshed after reading the words of this powerful man of God. Raheem Turane has opened a new door, a heavenly gateway to the understanding of relationships and I implore all who desire to experience a refreshing to walk through the door and enjoy your new journey in the biblical covenantal marriage relationship that God has designed for those He's called to the ministry of marriage.

Apostle Olivia Stith
Founder of TriManna School of the Prophets and Intercessors
Published author of:
"If God Is My Lover, Why Is My Bed So Cold?"
"Lord Is Boaz Lost Or Am I Just in the Wrong Field?"

Preface

Going through life, searching for the one who God has created for me I found myself in relationships with women who did not fit where God was taking me or could not fit where I was going. Through numerous relationships I have tried to make something happen out of myself without seeking God's approval, His wisdom, or His direction. Failing to do this has caused me to lose years in relationships that would not materialize anything positive but instead materialized hurt, pain, disappointment, lack of trust, insecurities, feelings of hopelessness, and low self-esteem… all because I tried to fit a rib in my body that was too small or too big to be housed in what God created in me.

In doing this I have suffered many failed relationships: a failed engagement and a failed marriage. Out of this, two beautiful children were produced who are engulfed in the dynamics of not doing it God's way. What exactly does that mean? I knew weeks before I got married that this was not the correct path for me. This was not what God was calling for me to do in that season. I knew that this was me covering up the fact that I was not over a failed engagement that was spawned by infidelity on both parts. Due to wanting people to feel and believe that I was over these hurt emotions, I entered into a relationship that God calls sacred disguised in a lie. I did not even love myself, therefore how could I love a person I had only known for ninety days?

You may be saying, "He's crazy"…and you are absolutely right. When you remove yourself so far from the will of God, you will medicate yourself with any and everything that will cause you to think that you are free when deep in your heart you know that you are truly bound. How can you love when you don't even love? How can you think straight when you don't think straight? How can you make decisions when you are indecisive?

I will tell you how: you trick yourself into believing that what you are doing has been sanctioned by God. In doing this you set yourself up to be a benefactor of all the repercussions of lying on God.

Your next thought or question may be, "Why would he write a book like this?" The answer is to prevent others who are searching to fill a void that no man or woman can, but only God can.

A couple years ago I was invited to speak at a Women's Retreat at the invitation of a thriving churches Women's department. The theme was "What Are You Harvesting?" and I was ecstatic about getting an opportunity to speak to this group of women because for some time the Lord had been dealing with me about the very topic of this book. I had only been divorced a little over a year and was quite surprised at having received such an invitation to speak. Who in the world would want to hear a message from a preacher who just had a public divorce? The man and woman of God no longer together? The talk of the town? Nevertheless I accepted the invitation and was excited about allowing the Lord to use me, the opportunity to start my healing process, and the road to redemption. Who says a Women's Retreat has to be just for women? This is not the level of redemption you may be thinking of, but the redemption that allows oneself to walk into their liberty and freedom.

On that day, I was there to meet the needs of five different demographics or groups of women that were in attendance. These groups consisted of the following:

- Group One: Married Women – These are women by definition who are newly married or those who have been married for years.

These individuals are in either thriving or struggling marriages. These are individuals who have gone through the legal and/or spiritual process of becoming one.

- Group Two: Divorced Women – These are women who were once married but for whatever reason find themselves in a place where they are no longer legally joined to the one they were legally bound to.

- Group Three: Engaged Women – These are women who believe they have found the one who has captured their heart and have the ability to be joined to that individual legally and/or spiritually as a spouse.

- Group Four: Widowed Women – These are the women who were married, however they lost their spouse due to death.

- Group Five: Single Women – This group can be divided into two sub-categories. Single Women A are the women who are not in a relationship, yet have the desire for that companionship and long for a partner. It is safe to note that a Single Woman A can be one who is in a relationship but there has been no expression of taking said relationship to the next level which some consider the engaged state. Then, there is Single Women B who are content with who they are in themselves and are not seeking nor desiring a mate.

Each group has specific needs, desires, and experiences. From the youngest to the oldest, they all desire to be wanted, loved, protected, considered, valued, and to receive and know what affection looks like and feels like.

Introduction

In order to understand what a man wants, we must get a good sense of who we are. When we find out who we are, we find out what he needs. Let's look at the first man and woman:

In Genesis 2:18-21, we see Moses saying as follows:

"18 And the Lord God said, 'It is not good that the man should be alone; I will make him a helpmeet for him. 19 And out of the ground the Lord God formed every beast of the field, and every fowl of the air; and brought them unto Adam to see what he will call them; and whatsoever Adam called every living creature, that was the name thereof. 20 And Adam gave names to all cattle, and to all the fowl of the air, and to every beast of the field; but for Adam there was not found a helpmeet for him. 21 And the Lord God caused a deep sleep to

fall upon Adam and he slept; and He took one of his ribs, and closed up the flesh instead thereof..." (KJV)

Carefully read Verses 19-20 again: we see God continuing to work, but wait! Didn't God just say in Verse 18 that man (Adam) should not be alone? Now He's making and creating animals? Are we not more important than the animals? Isn't it our desire to have companionship? God promised a woman, a wife, and helpmeet...but then made him wait? Why? Why would God make man wait for his woman?

God makes man wait for the woman because God wanted man to complete his God-assignment first. God-assignment? What do you mean "God-assignment"? This is where many men make a mistake and end up obtaining something before the proper time. Adam had an assignment to do and until Adam completed his assignment that God had for him he was ineligible to receive the spoken word of God concerning the appearance of his helpmeet (wife).

What does this mean ladies? This means if Adam cannot wait to complete the process that God has assigned for his life, he is spiritually ineligible to make you his wife. Why is this? Through the process of naming the animals, God was exercising Adam's ability to complete an assignment prior to reaping the rewards of completion. If God had allowed Adam to skip the process and moved straight to his reward (his helpmeet), Adam would have named his helpmeet something that she was not.

Genesis 2:19-20c: "19 And out of the ground the Lord God formed every beast of the field, and every fowl of the air; and brought them unto Adam to see what he will call them; and whatsoever Adam called every living creature, that was the name thereof. 20 And

Adam gave names to all cattle, and to all the fowl of the air, and to every beast of the field;" (KJV)

God was testing Adam. Why would Moses write in Genesis 2:20d the following:

20d "But for Adam there was not found a helpmeet for him."

Once again, it appears as though the animals are receiving preferential treatment over the image of God, but why is this? God knows that the animals will continue to worship and praise Him. Regardless of anything, they will do exactly what God created them to do.

However, because God breathed the breath of life into Adam, God wanted to make something specific to himself: an image out of His image. God did not want Adam to name Woman something she was not supposed to be named. So God used a test, or exercise, to strengthen Adam's ability to appropriately name what he saw.

I wish I had known this when I was married. Maybe I could have named some stuff right. I repeat, IF I HAD KNOWN THIS WHEN I GOT MARRIED, I WOULD HAVE NAMED SOME STUFF RIGHT. Your husband or future husband has the ability to name what he sees, therefore if he does not operate in this then he is not operating in his God-assigned authority granted in Genesis 2:19-20.

Take a moment and declare to yourself: I am Ruth. I am Ruth. I am Ruth. I AM RUTH. There is so much power in declaring something that God himself even utilizes it. Since we are created in His image and in His likeness and have His spirit breathed within us, we have the same ability to say "Let there be light" and light should appear. We have the same ability to say "Let there be a firmament" and there must be a firmament. We have the same ability to say "Let the waters be separated from dry land" and it must happen.

In understanding who we are, we see in Genesis 2:21 the first surgery, the first anesthesia, and the first person created after creation. Woman's spirit was already created prior to a physical body being produced.

Genesis 1:26 "26 And God said, let us make man in our image, after our likeness; and let them have dominion over the fish of the sea, and over the fowl of the air, and over the cattle and over all the earth, and over every creeping thing that creepeth upon the earth." (KJV)

The word "them" means you were already thought of: God just wanted the male (man) to do all of the work. Your spirit was present through all of this. You have just as much creative ability and power as the man. How is this possible? Reexamine Genesis 2:20 where it states "And Adam gave names". In Adam you were. To this day, man continues this test. What does that mean? Man continues this test when he wakes up and sees woman every morning. When we examine Genesis 2:21, we see Adam was put to sleep. He was in an unconscious state, however when Adam woke up or was conscious in Genesis 2:23 not only did Adam recognize that something happened to him physically, but he also recognized that there was someone who looked like himself. Adam also recognized that she was physically different. This is what caused him to declare what he saw. When he declared what he saw that was in front of him, not only did he speak her into existence but he also told her who she was when he declared "she shall be called Woman because she was taken out of man" (Genesis 2:23d, KJV). When we examine Genesis 2:25, we learn they were naked and not ashamed. Moses, the writer of Genesis, is not speaking of their physical appearance, rather he is speaking to their ability to be vulnerable with one another.

It should be acceptable for your husband or potential mate to cry in front of you. It should be acceptable for him to share his issues because he is being vulnerable. The day that Adam did not protect Eve's vulnerability is the day they recognized each other's flaws and were expelled from their perfect place in God. In Genesis 3:1-7, Moses tells us:

"1 Now the serpent was more subtitle than any beast of the field which the Lord God had made. And he said unto the woman, Yea, hath God said, ye shall not eat of every tree of the garden? 2 And the woman said unto the serpent, We may eat of the fruit of the trees of the garden; 3 But the fruit of the tree which is in the midst of the garden, God hath said, Ye shall not eat of it, neither shall ye touch it, lest ye die. 4 And the serpent said unto the woman, Ye shall not surely die; 5 For God doth know that in the day ye eat thereof, then your eyes

shall be opened, and ye shall be as gods, knowing good and evil. 6 And when the woman saw that the tree was good for food, and that it was pleasant to the eyes, and the tree to be desired to make one wise, she took of the fruit thereof, and did eat, and gave also unto her husband with her; and he did eat. 7 And the eyes of them both were opened, and they knew that they were naked; and they sewed fig leaves together and make themselves aprons." (KJV)

Knowing that this serpent was more subtle than any of the beasts of the field which the Lord had made lets us know that there were other opportunities to relinquish their vulnerabilities, but Adam protected his wife. I could imagine Adam being so confident in his wife's abilities to ward off partial truths being spoken to her, not realizing that his covering and presence added strength in weak places. Thus a partial truth and a back seat caused the one whom he daily spoke words of affirmation for to fall prey to a partial truth in his presence. Adam knew the truth but was afraid to speak it, knowing that if the one he constantly affirmed would not listen that God would have wiped Eve out. His love for her, so deep and binding, caused Adam to willingly partake of a partial truth because he remembered everything he experienced when he did not have her: the loneliness, the constant reminder that even the animals that were not created in the image of God nor His likeness had a mate, and the idea that he would be the only one of his kind. He willingly relinquished his authority as a protector to become a partaker of a partial truth which opened both he and his wife to a new realm of seeing each other outside the eyes of God.

    With this willful exercise, man lost all sensitivity to what and whom God has assigned and granted for their lives. This prompts the necessity for both parties to recognize the need for each other. We see the ideal reconciliation of a relationship in the book of Ruth…

Notes

1

A Woman Who Knows Where to Place Her Friends

Friends can be a killer in a marriage. It does not matter to us if you have been best friends forever or two days prior to marrying us. If we sense danger or something is not right with your friend, we will be vocal and express our feelings regarding it. I believe that it is safe to say that sometime in your present or past experiences, there are about 20-30% of you who are reading this book who have experienced issues where a friend or friends have come in the way of your love life. You know the stories, you know the conversations you have: "Girrrrrl, he is no good!" "My man does it THIS way!" "Chiiiild, he's a dog!" Shall I go on?

Even if this is true, you are the selector or the recipient of what you allow. If your man is a "dog" or he is "no good", then there is something in you or your external relationships that causes an internal conflict. What does this mean?

We know that individuals with self-esteem issues tend to find themselves in relationships with other individuals who do not build them up because they feel unworthy of being built up. However, these same individuals tend to gravitate to the ones who make them comfortable in a place where they have not resolved their own internal issues. Thus pushing away the individual who has the ability to pull you out of your low place and set you to where you need to be.

In most cases, your friends may be absolutely right. In other cases, your friends can be so envious of the potential man you have that they will do anything to derail your coming out of a place that they are in themselves. They are afraid that if you get "free" from that place that they will no longer be of need and become irrelevant in your life because you have outgrown where they are.

A friend of mine was in the process of getting married to an older woman a few years ago. His family continually talked down about this woman because she has children out of wedlock and she rarely had them because they would be with her parents. They talked about the appearance of the children when they interacted with the children: why did these babies never have any name brand clothes and sneakers? Why was this little girls' hair never done? They expressly told my friend that this woman was not the one for him. When he would bring her around, they would give her the cold shoulder making her feel unwelcomed and like she did not belong. They would smile in her face and as soon as she would leave, they would talk about her as if she were nothing. It got to be so bad that my friend began to second guess what he expressed God had commanded him to do. Even up to his wedding rehearsal, his family was attempting to make every available resource for him to escape a marriage he desired but that they did not want for him.

On the day of the wedding, everyone pretended as though everything was just fine. But as the family sat in the reception hall, they talked loudly and placed bets on how long this relationship would last. Blessedly, my friend did not hear this and as he and his bride danced the night away. I took the liberty to speak with those who were making these comments and informed them that their words have the ability to create an opportunity for confusion to come in and to destroy not just their lives, but the lives of everyone who was connected to their present and their future.

A few years later, this same couple found themselves in the fight of their life for their marriage and the same family members who were placing bets and speaking of the downfall of this union was making it easy for my friend to run away from his newly made family. The young woman had her own internal issues: some things followed her from her past, some challenges and issues she never dealt with. These are the things that crept up because she had friends, too. Her friends were speaking and illuminating every shortcoming of her husband and offering an environment conducive to walking away.

This couple became bitter and their closest friends including preachers and people in their communities were making that one statement we all hate to hear: I told you so. This caused the love they once shared to fall prey to the pride that laid dormant in their hearts; it finally woke up.

There were a few of us who spoke the truth, who examined both sides, who heard from God and encouraged this couple to fight for what they stated in front of us all and in the sight of God that He joined together, that either

God said it or they lied on His name. Which was the answer?

They were apart for a few months, they fought for a few months, they hurt each other for a few months; but when they recognized that it was the people, or the subtle serpent, that was telling a partial truth, and they gradually put their pride to the side and submitted to the will of God in their lives.

In the Book of Ruth 1:12-14 we read the following:

"12 Turn again, my daughters, go your way; for I am too old to have a husband. If I should say, I have hope, if I should have a husband also tonight, and should also bear sons; 13 Would ye tarry for them 'til they were grown? would ye stay for them from having husbands? nay my daughters; for it grieveth me much for your sakes that the hands of the Lord is gone out against me. 14 And they lifted up their voices, and wept

again; and Orpah kissed her mother in law; but Ruth clave to her." (KJV)

Ruth had a relationship with Orpah in that they came from the same community; they came from the same environment, were raised under the same rules, and they very well could have been related before becoming sisters-in-law. According to Ruth 1:2-7 (KJV), Orpah was married to Chilion and Ruth was married to Mahlon who were both the sons of Elimelech and Naomi. First, Elimelech passes leaving Naomi with two sons and her daughters-in-law. Next, Chilion and Mahlon die leaving three women with no male to support nor protect them. Naomi gives her daughters-in-law an opportunity to go back to the environment that her sons found them in, hoping that they would be able to find another husband of their own.

How many women today could honestly say that they would leave everything behind that they know, everything they are comfortable with, everything that promotes a healthy state of mind for them at the moment to wander off with their mother-in-law? I beseech the married women to take a moment right now and imagine if your husband passed away tomorrow (God forbid).

What would be your first instinct? Would you want to return to what is familiar or would you set up a new home with his mother?

We watch Orpah make the decision to go back to what is familiar for her and many times in life we go back to places that have no ability to produce or to incubate who we have become when we have left and wind up killing us or ostracizing us when we return. Ruth knew that going back with Orpah was not the right thing to do. She trusted what she (Ruth) wanted more than what she knew was awaiting her if she followed behind her friend.

Her friend (Orpah) was in the same boat as her, not having anything or any means to support herself. She lost her resources, she lost her comfort, she lost her protection, but Ruth refused to continue down the same path that Orpah was heading because she recognized the importance of breaking the cycle that was known in their community. This cycle was that women who did not have husbands were relegated to being sexually mishandled by other men because they had no protection. They became beggars, prostitutes, and anything else they needed to be in order to survive.

I believe a part of Ruth really missed the family that she had left behind in Moab, but she understood that the day she was given in marriage she was no longer the responsibility of her family, namely her father. If her father was dead, her brothers would have the ultimate say regarding her existence. Ruth was willing to take a chance and hope that her mother-in-law Naomi would become pregnant again because the new son would become her husband once he came of age, making him legally responsible to provide for her regardless of the age of Ruth. She operated in a level of faith whereas Orpah operated in a level of selfishness in hopes that she could bypass the rules that were established for a widow.

It is important to note that God made us relational beings. In being relational, it means that each man and woman has the need or desire for friendship and companionship. A woman who does not have any friends automatically raises a red flag to her potential mate because it causes the mate to be things that he does not have the ability to be.

Many times we expect our spouse to be our best friend. Theoretically your spouse should be your best friend, but you need someone outside of your spouse to talk to, spend time with, and relate to. It is important to state that this individual be the same sex. This individual should be a person who has more to lose than you. An individual who has nothing to lose will cause damage, chaos, confusion, and conflict because they have not attained the level or lifestyle that you are in. These are the individuals that will cosign foolishness, nonsense, a way of escape, and an alternative lifestyle. Be aware of single friends who have nothing. These are the ones who are watching, envying, and secretly desiring the very thing that you have while pondering how they are going to obtain it. Their happiness is in your misery.

A mentor is a person who has a level of experience and has obtained a level of possessions that far exceeds and trumps where you are and where you have been. A mentor is a mature individual who will challenge your inexperience while encouraging you in love to assist in avoiding the traps and tricks that they have already been through. A mentor is one who has been tried and tested in the areas that have the potential of causing the weakest individuals to give up prematurely when they are on the verge of a successful breakthrough. A mentor is a person who sits back and observes challenges of individuals but are not ones who go seeking; they are the ones who are sought after.

In 2nd Kings 2:9, we find Elijah, the mentor, about to return to the Lord and leaving Elisha, his mentee, behind to carry on everything that he was shown by Elijah. It is now Elisha's time to walk. He has been given every counsel possible, every tool to be successful. Elisha watched his mentor speak and marveled at the things that would come to pass. He would hear Elijah speak to and counsel kings. He also saw how outsiders envied the relationship he had with Elijah (2nd Kings 2:5). However, this did not cause Elisha's attention to be moved off of what he was receiving from his mentor. Many times within our lives there are jealous individuals who envy our God-sent relationships. Individuals who attempt to pull apart these relationships because in reality they want it for themselves, they just are not bold enough to obtain it legally. We have all had people in our lives who would do anything to pull apart a relationship that caused them to be obsolete and unimportant. We should note that when you know that your mentor has been sent by God, there is a blessing in submitting to the authority that God has placed you under. When you rightfully submit, all of the naysayers will see the blessing that God has sent your way.

We see in 2nd Kings 2:15 that when the mentor/mentee relationship was over, we see the very individuals who were jealous now coming to Elisha to recognize that he truly received the mantle from his mentor Elijah. This caused them to bow down to Elisha in recognition that they were wrong for not submitting to their own mentors. Elisha was utilized as an example to show us what real mentorship looks like and what real mentorship produces: a blessing.

In walking with Elijah, Elisha was granted what he asked for which was the ability to do twice as much as his mentor. Elisha's faithfulness granted him the ability to be blessed by his mentor, but God also granted the desire that Elijah wanted to give to his mentee (2nd Kings 2:10).

Every man wants a woman who knows where to place her friends. Every man wants a woman who understands balance, boundaries, and privacy. As it is our job to protect our home from intruders, and it is just as much your job to protect the relationship from intruders.

Notes

Notes

2

A Woman Who Knows the Value of Holding On

Many times in life, we give up because it seems hard. The human mind always reflects and goes back to the last experience that is similar to what we are currently going through. Many times we give up too soon and in the mix of giving up too soon we lose out on the ability to be our biggest and greatest blessing. In giving up, we have no idea of the magnitude of what we could truly obtain if we just waited a little while longer. Waiting seems to be the most difficult thing that humans have to do. This is a day and age where we do not have to wait for food to be cooked because we can walk into a restaurant and it is already made. This is a day and age where we do not even have to go to the library to read a book because we can pull it up on our phone. This is a day and age where we have made the process of waiting so obsolete that even our children have tantrums because what they are expecting, they are not getting at the very moment they desire it.

Waiting.

By definition it means "the action of staying where one is or delaying action until a particular time or until something else happens". That in itself says a whole lot when it is broken down.

"The action of staying where one is" – Being married for all the wrong reasons and being fearful of all the words of truth that may have been spoken concerning my blatant lie on God stating that I should have been married. I worried more than anything about what people would say over what I felt in my heart. Could you imagine driving home every day and sitting in your driveway getting yourself together for over 45 minutes because you did not know what you would experience when you walk in your door? Have you ever felt a sense of needing to escape because if you did not, you felt like you would lose it? Have you ever experienced the internal struggle of knowing that you are dying inside? This is not just a physical death, but it is an emotional and spiritual death as well. You are losing the sensitivity that connects your heart to reality. You are losing your spiritual connection which causes you to lose faith because you are not hearing God speak. Have you ever felt so mentally consumed that even when you slept at night your mind was still racing, processing, and pondering? Have you ever felt so hopeless that you wanted to end your life just to escape this place you are in? Maybe not. But there are too many people who have.

"Delaying action" – Have you ever been in a place where you needed to make a move but fear gripped you and your feet felt trapped in cement? You can see where you want to be, the destination you are trying to get to, your arms are pumping, your thighs are attempting to pull you forward, but you are confined to the small space that is your current location. Your heart is racing, feeling as though the walls are caving in all because it is right in your grasp, it is right in your view…but the weight which is hidden fear of the unknown, the possibilities causes you to stay in a location longer than you are supposed to. You do not realize that this delayed evacuation causes more pressure, more pain, more anxiety, more hurt, and more indecisiveness. This place has caused even the most well-rounded, educated, physically attractive, got-it-going-on individual to lose everything like the breath being knocked out of them when being unexpectedly punched in the chest. This level of waiting has caused genocides. This level of waiting has caused societal turmoil that has been documented in the confines of history. You would think that because we have references that we would not go through these same situations again, but for some reason they continue to happen every single day.

"Something else happening" – You thought overlooking being belittled would stop once it was confronted, but it continued to happen. It went from being in the privacy of your bedroom to being in front of the congregation of your church. You thought it would go no further than the congregation of your church, but it reared its head at a corporate event. Enough is enough. I do not care who gets upset; no one has seen my private pain. No one has seen the tears I have cried. No one has heard the thoughts I have had. It is time for me to find me.

What is the value of waiting? What is the value of holding on? According to Mark 5:25-34, we are provided an account of a woman who had an issue with blood. Let me explain what it means that this woman had an "issue with blood". Every female, once they get to an appropriate age, has something called a menstrual cycle. Normally, this menstrual cycle can last anywhere from 21-35 days in adults and from 21-45 days in young teens. The bleeding portion of this menstrual cycle can last anywhere from 2 to 7 days and this is called menstruation. This unidentified woman had this issue for twelve years straight. She had been to all of the doctors, she had gone to every specialist, she has tried every remedy, but nothing seemed to work for her. She could not go into the synagogues anymore which caused her to be cut off from any spiritual growth. She could not be around people because of the stench of continually bleeding. Even in the midst of her struggling, she did not give up. She kept believing that one day something would happen and she would no longer have this issue. Mark informs us that as Jesus was walking he was thronged by thousands of people. Everyone was touching him. He was being touched by men. He was being touched by women. He was being touched by children. However, this woman who barely had the strength to stand up straight from having daily cramps for twelve years not only found herself bowed over but also found herself crawling on her hands and knees in hopes that if she could get to Jesus something would happen for her.

Could you imagine how this woman had to have been stepped on, her attire being trampled and snagged by the multitude of feet? Can you see her looking back in desperation looking up to those who are well-bodied and abled? All she wanted was to touch the hem of his garment. She was not going to allow an unintentional delay to stop her from crawling on her hands and knees. I can imagine that there were dogs out there as well as any other animal that had the ability to crawl, vying for the same position that she was in.

This woman who knew the value of holding on knew that she was not going to allow anything to stop her. She finally touches the garment of Christ and Mark lets us know that upon her touching him, her issue immediately dries up. This causes Jesus to stop everything because he recognized that something was taken from Him. Were there not hundreds, if not thousands of people out there touching him? Did he not know that things that things were being taken from Him? Of course He did. However, what He was giving away paled in comparison to what was taken from Him.

Jesus stops and screams, "Who touched my clothes?" He could not see who took something from him. This prompted him to ask the question again.

"Who touched me?" This causes Jesus to look around because what He saw did not match what He lost. The woman was fearful because she felt that she was wrong for receiving her miracle. When Jesus recognized her, He tells her that her faith has caused her to be made whole. She was determined that since she was there, she was going to hold on to Him until He recognized that it was her. This means that even when it does not look the way you want it to look, you have to have the faith to believe that if God is present in a situation that He can and will make something happen. Jesus does not curse her, He sends her in peace, and removes her issue.

Growing up I was told of a relative of mine who we affectionately called a "Rolling Stone" but for all purposes here, we will call him "Uncle L". He had issues which were small to him but huge to our family. He loved the women and I would love to hear the many stories of him from his young days. Don't judge me, this was before I found Christ, but I would love to hear stories about how he could just go places and command the attention of all the women.

The grin on his face, the confident strut he presented, and even his physical appearance made me in my pre-pubescent mind want to be just like him. He stayed with the freshest car: a black Lincoln, two-door coupe. I remember going past his house and tapping on his window to see if he was home; he always had some fine woman over there and his house smelled like weed. He called himself schooling me on how to interact with women and twenty plus years later I can honestly say that this is one of the reasons I could have had so much trouble with the opposite sex.

Did I tell you that Uncle L was married with two daughters? I loved my aunt and my cousins, but I could not understand how my uncle was able to maintain somewhat of a "playhouse" that I had never seen them in. I mainly went by his "playhouse" because I knew he would give me money and the chances of me seeing some sexy woman were extremely high.

Now to get back to my saved self: my aunt was beautiful in my sight and opinion. She rarely talked, but she could surely cook. I wonder if she knew what he was doing. There were times when I would mention that I saw my uncle and then I would quickly change the subject. My aunt acted like she never heard these mistakes, but I knew she did. Her eyes would gloss over, she would change the subject herself, and even make comments about how Uncle L was always working. I wondered if she knew about the "playhouse", but if she did she never said anything. It was a little odd that she never came around for big family functions and this was a shame because I must reiterate, the woman could cook. She also gave the best gifts. What was she not giving to my uncle?

Later on in life, the secret came out that my uncle had another daughter by a woman who lived in my neighborhood. You may wonder how I found out. Well, everyone knows those big mouth kids in the neighborhood. They were more than joyful to point out another pretty girl who looked identical to my uncle's other daughters with his exact face and ask me, "Don't you know that's your cousin over there?!" There was a huge fight in the neighborhood. My family meant everything to me.

One day after that I went to the "playhouse". At this time Uncle L was not doing too well. There were murmurs in the family that he was addicted to crack. I had no qualms about asking him and sadly he confirmed the rumors of those same big mouth children. You can imagine how shocked I was, but I still loved him.

Maybe that was why my aunt always looked like that.

As we all grew older, this newfound cousin was integrated into family functions and my aunt who was never present all of a sudden made an appearance at every gathering. I really did not care that much but after having a conversation with my aunt, she explained the situation. She told me that when everyone was encouraging her to leave her marriage, she saw something more in my uncle than he saw in himself. Let me tell you about him today.

Uncle L is drug free, alcohol free, "playhouse" free, and he is an active deacon in his church. I wonder what would have happened if my aunt would have left him. Would he still be on drugs? Would he be on the streets? Would he be in the grave?

My aunt reminds me of Ruth who understood that even in her tears, even in the ripping, even in the humiliation, and even in the uncertainty that she had to hold on to what she knew was right. Even though she was torn, she understood holding on to her faith, holding on to believing that God will make a way, that God will provide, and that God will turn it around in her favor.

Ruth 1:14d states that "Ruth clave unto her (Naomi)" (KJV), showing that Ruth loved her mother-in-law dearly. She loved her so much that she was willing to disassociate herself from her past and was willing to embrace anew. Ruth recognized the importance and the value of all the things her mother-in-law poured into her. Could you imagine the conversations that they had prior to Ruth marrying Mahlon? Could you imagine the special the secrets that she shared about her son? Could you imagine the words of encouragement that she was given? Could you imagine the correction that he has been given by her mother-in-law who now has no one? Ruth was sensitive to the emotion of loneliness. She knew that by leaving her mother-in-law she would be just as empty as the one who lost her husband and her two sons. In knowing this, Ruth did not want her mother-in-law to suffer another level of death that she would have had to take on from having someone that she loved and cared for leaving her.

Orpah relinquished the blessing by going back home. When she went back home, she showed her mother-in-law that there was nothing else that she could offer her. Ruth recognized that even if Naomi could not produce another son, as long as she had her mother-in-law she had a connection with her husband.

Every man wants a woman who understands the importance of holding on. Every man wants a woman who values waiting, staying, enduring, and believing. Every man wants a woman who will continue to love him in spite of where he currently is.

Notes

Notes

3

A Woman with Wisdom and Discernment

In life we draw from past experiences when it comes to what we should or should not do. We draw from the experiences of others and what we have heard, however in the midst of using our own knowledge and experience we have the ability to forfeit and abort a bigger picture. Wisdom and discernment without God is really flesh and humanistic thinking.

We allow our minds to create a reality and we make attempts to make our world fit into the reality that we have created. An example would be a person who is schizophrenic: they create an alternate world to escape traumatic events. We all have these moments. Some of us have been abused to the point where we push it so far back in our minds that we try to hide from it. You hear a certain song and your mind instantly goes back and replays the events of him walking out on you. You smell a certain cologne and your mind gravitates back to the time where your uncle put his hands down your pants while permeating the same scent.

Our mind is a giant computer which collects and stores masses of data. Some things pop up at the most inopportune time and some things stay at the forefront of the monitor in your head. These are the things that you have daily use of. These are the things that if that file was lost you would not be able to function. Some of us have become so accustomed to opening these files that we refuse to put them in the recycle bin where they belong.

According to Ruth 1:16-17, we see Ruth begging her mother-in-law for her not to be forced into going back to Moab. Ruth made a declaration that wherever Naomi went, she would follow; wherever Naomi lived, Ruth would live; whoever Naomi's people were, they would also be Ruth's people; that whoever Naomi worshipped as God, she too would worship; and lastly, that wherever Naomi died, that is where Ruth would die, too. Ruth knew what she faced if she went back and stayed in Moab and many times we go back to what is familiar to us and never become recipients of a greater level of freedom than where we are because we remember the comforts of home and what we think it will be like when we go back.

This has caused many of us to be put in tight spots because we remember the former, and with remembering the former we believe it has the ability to care for us in our current state. With making this bad decision we go back to a place that lacks the ability to support who we have become. This forces us to make a decision to either struggle through who we are now or go back to an old place, an old mindset, and an old way of doing things when we have already outgrown those places. We are picking up garments that no longer fit us and this causes us to be seen as though we are crazy or that we made a wrong decision with leaving in the first place.

There once was a man who outgrew a pair of shoes, but these shoes were the most expensive shoes that could be bought. They were a limited edition. He wore them every day, received compliments, people asked him where he bought them, and the man would keep this information hidden because he did not want anyone to have what he had. As time progressed, the wear and tear of the heels and the soles of these shoes became so worn down that he could not wear them anymore. His feet began to grow and he no longer wore the same size. Yet everyday this man would fantasize about wearing these shoes. One day while out walking, he found a cobbler who had a sign advertising "Shoe Restoration". This was exciting news to the man! He had thoughts in his head about how soon he could get his favored shoes to the cobbler.

When he brought the shoes in, the cobbler stated, "These shoes can't be repaired."

The man pleaded with the cobbler and the cobbler finally agreed to repair the shoes. The one thing the man failed to report to the cobbler was that his feet had grown.

Each day the man would go by the cobbler's establishment to check on the progress of his beloved shoes. Finally, the cobbler presented him with the newly restored, newly shined shoes. The man was ecstatic. He pulled his other shoes off and attempted to put his foot in the shoes he loved. As he tried and tried, he realized that his foot would not fit.

He looked at the cobbler in distress, asking him, "What did you do to my shoes?!"

The cobbler replied, "I did what you told me, sir! I put new heels and new soles, and stitched them back up, just like you asked!"

The man broke down and cried in his frustration.

The cobbler pondered what he could do and asked the man how else he could help.

The man replied, "I just want to wear these shoes!"

But the cobbler stated, "With the type of material these shoes are made up, there is nothing we can do. I am sorry, sir. It is time to get new shoes in the right size."

Many times we want something so badly that we are willing to cause harm to ourselves to get something that we have outgrown. The apostle Paul tells us in Philippians 3:13e-14 about "forgetting those things which are behind and reaching forth unto those things which are before, I press toward the mark of the high calling of God in Christ Jesus" (KJV) and Ruth understood that in order for her to remove herself from her past of being an idol worshipping Moabite she was willing to take on the wisdom that she received from her mother-in-law, Naomi. Ruth discerned that the God that Naomi served was the true God. She understood that her past of being a widow would not cause her to never be married again. Ruth knew that she had to do something that was so uncommon that it would force the hand of God to look past who she was by birth to seeing who she will be.

Every man wants a woman who has enough wisdom to navigate their way through life's challenges and circumstances. Every man wants a woman with enough foresight that they can see past what they do not have, where they are not, to seeing who they will be. In so many words, we want a woman who is absolutely confident in who she is.

Notes

Notes

4

A Woman Who Isn't Afraid of Work

There was a time when it was frowned upon for a woman to work outside of the home. It was unacceptable for a man to allow his wife to do any external domestic work outside of the home. He would have been shunned in his community if it was discovered that his wife had a career. Outside of being a widow, it was socially inappropriate.

The jobs that these women would hold would typically be jobs that will hide them; these women would not be seen in the public eye. They would be maids in hotels, secretaries for men: they would be put in places where they would not be seen because it was socially unacceptable.

This did not change until WWII when our entire country was forced to join together and every American had to pull the weight and burden of war. Let's think about this: WWII began September 1, 1939. That is only 77.5 years ago! Even after proving themselves to be dedicated members of our society through their hard-working efforts to keep our country afloat during a tragic war, women were still not a stable force in the workplace.

During the 1950s, women were still mostly relegated to the home to raise children which were born to them after the soldiers came back from war. They returned to the domestic work to which they were accustomed. It was not until the late 1960s when they were finally able to escape from a domesticated home life for a second time and enter the workforce at increased rates, much to the dismay of many.

In 2017, there is a heightened importance of everyone working. This includes, but is not limited to, a 9-5, five days a week, 26 pay cycles in a calendar year job which is necessary within the economic climate we live in. It does not matter to us if you are flipping fries or you are the Chief Executive Officer of a small business or a Fortune 500 company. Every man desires a woman who is not afraid to work.

There was a young couple from the Young Adult Ministry where I previously pastored who no one believed would make it. People would talk down about the young man and would reference his family and how his parents lived in the homeless shelter and how his sisters always looked unkempt. People would talk about how he has a sex demon on him, that he was not going anywhere in life, and that the young woman could do better. The young man did not have the ideal job making major dollars, instead he was working at a gas station for a little above minimum wage. One thing that no one ever paid attention to was his work ethic and dedication.

Now, I will agree that I did not like some of the things he was doing, but what I will say is that he had a heart for God and he was going to live past the expectations and limitations that people placed on him.

I remember the day this young couple came to my office to share with me that the young lady had gotten pregnant.

I WENT OFF.

When I finally calmed down, I asked him what his plan is. He stated to me, "Pastor Rah, I'm going to make this right".

I embraced both of these young people and told them we will make it through this.

This young lady was a workaholic. Not only did she complete school, she worked two jobs and had a side hustle of styling hair. The baby came and still no marriage proposal.

I continued to observe from a distance and less than a year later we were back for Meeting #2. A second pregnancy was on the table and the discussion from the couple revolved around adoption and abortion.

I made an agreement with them: if they did not have an abortion, I would be willing to adopt their baby and they would have full parental rights. I promised to maintain the baby financially until they became stable. They decided to think about it.

A year later, the baby is here and they get married. The young lady continued through school, maintained her side hustle, and now finds herself working at a major hospital in the United States.

Why am I telling you this story?

In spite of every obstacle and every challenge that she personally faced, she refused to allow her circumstances to prevent her from being able to financially support herself and her family.

How many of us would go into a strange land, experience difficult opposition, and work amongst people we do not know or give up on situations because it does not look like what we think it should be or what other people think it should look like?

By listening to what other people have said, we miss out on the blessing because it is not what people say we should have.

To date, this couple is happily married with an additional baby which they planned together to complete their family. They are living in a house, they have cars which are paid off, and they are living in overflow. Those who stated that their marriage would not last are now divorced and bitter, fighting like individuals who have never experienced the power, presence, and the liberty of God.

This couple understood that as long as they work together, nothing is impossible through God. Those who gave up and divorced discovered that everything is possible without God.

According to Ruth 2:2-3 states: "And Ruth the Moabitess said unto Naomi, Let me now go to the field, and glean ears of corn after him in whose sight I shall find grace. And she said unto her, Go, my daughter. And she went, and came, and gleaned in the field after the reapers: and her hap was to light on a part of the field belonging unto Boaz, who was of the kindred of Elimelech". (KJV) Ruth was not afraid to go to a new place where she did not know anyone. She was not afraid of being an outsider. Due to her lack of fear and lack of pride, she did not allow herself to refuse working a menial job because she knew there was a bigger picture. There was something that needed to be done that far exceeded what she did not want to do.

Her obedience was setting her up for a miracle.

Many times, God will place us in a position where we may have to be the breadwinner in order to save our families. Men love a woman who is not afraid to do some dirty work for the betterment of the family.

Our obedience in doing what God tells us to do is also setting us up for a miracle.

Let's look at this from a spiritual aspect: every man wants a woman who is not only afraid to work at a physical job, but every man wants a woman who is not afraid of spiritual work.

Let me make this clear: every man wants a woman with whom he is spiritually yoked. Amos 3:3 states, "How can two walk together, except they be agreed?" (KJV). Within the covenant of a God-perceived relationship, it is imperative that this conversation is had at the onset. Yes, we should talk about finances! Yes, we should talk about children! Yes, we should talk about where we are going to live! Yes, we should talk about extended family members! However, the most overlooked area is the work of the ministry. Where do I fit? How will it work? Who is called?

Where do I fit you might ask?

Moses gets a revelation in Genesis 2:24 that states, "Therefore shall a man leave his father and his mother and shall cleave unto his wife and they shall be one flesh" (KJV). When marrying an individual, whether a woman marrying a man or a man marrying a woman, there are no longer two separate entities, but instead one individual in the eyesight of God. You may not be the one with a title or hold an office within a church, however when God sees you, he sees the one who has the title and who has the office. There is no escaping the joining together of two individuals.

This is where the enemy wreaks the most havoc within a marriage or a pre-marriage. When we fail to understand that we are either the male version or the female version of one another, we fail to realize that in my spouse I was, and because I was in my spouse, I also have the title and hold the office. Even though I may not function within the title or the office, I still have it because it is yoked to my spouse.

How will it work?

Paul tells us in Ephesians 5:22, "Wives, submit yourselves unto your own husbands, as unto the Lord" (KJV). Paul gives us a comparative clause by stating "as unto the Lord". In the Greek, there are two different types of comparative clauses. 1) *Elucidation* which means that wives are to give their husbands the same unquestioned, absolute submission they give to Christ (KJV). 2) *Emphasis* which means that wives are to submit to their husbands as submission rendered by them truly is submission rendered to Christ himself (KJV).

In so many words, when the wife yields her will to that of her husband, she yields to the Lord provided the husband's directions are in the fear of God and/or in line with God's will for their lives.

Who was called?

Moses clearly provides one of the most evasive answers in the Bible. Better yet, the church has done a poor job of educating its' congregants and families pertaining to who is called in ministry when one is already operating in their gift.

Moses attains a Levitical revelation from God as to who is called into the ministry. We read in Exodus 30:30, "And thou shalt anoint Aaron and his sons and consecrate them, that they may minister unto me in the priests' office" (KJV), thus informing us that the whole family is called into the ministry. Aaron was first called, but God did not want just Aaron. He wanted the entire family.

Many of you may be reading this and say, "Well, I see his sons being called, but not his wife!"

We need to note once again that God does not separate us when he sees us. He sees our bloodline and those attached to it.

Exodus 29:9d states, "And the priests' office shall be theirs for a perpetual statute and thou shall consecrate Aaron and his sons" (KJV), letting us know that the priesthood was going to continually run through the bloodline of Aaron.

Now as we look at Amos 3:3, we have a clear understanding of where we fit, how it will work, and who is called. When we fail to have these conversations, we will find that it is easier to be yoked in fleshly things than in Godly things. We can be yoked in the bedroom because we both like freaky stuff. We can be yoked in our spending habits because neither of us enjoy saving money. We can be yoked in the way we raise our children because we both believe in not sparing the rod. We can be yoked in household chores because we both like a clean house. We can be yoked in education because we both want to better ourselves through school. We can be yoked in our communication habits because we both know how to articulate ourselves.

Amos is talking to us about agreement and many times based upon our upbringing, community, culture, experiences, values, and morals we may not understand the power in agreement.

For example, as a Black man coming from New York City, a friendly face could often be perceived as a threat, whereas an individual raised in the South may see a friendly face as good upbringing. Although we live in the same country, our perceptions and experiences are different and therefore procure different responses.

The power of disagreement is responsible for destroying plenty of marriages within the church which is the reason the divorce rate among believers is the equivalent or higher than that of unbelievers. Let me give you a real life example:

Back in 2009, I was the Youth/Young Adult Pastor of a small church located in Virginia. I was heavily relied upon to move this demographic to their desired and destined place in God. In doing such, I was able to gain the hearts, love, and respect of those who actively participated and those who minimally participated. This love grew from a pastoral love to that of a father loving his many children. I recognized their individual gifts and began releasing them to operate within their assigned callings. The ministry began to swell with more youth so that the young adult demographic outgrew the rest of the body. As we began to receive rapid growth, the spotlight was placed upon me more and more from when we first began.

My spouse at the time participated and would attend Youth/Young Adult Bible Study with me. I would be remiss if I did not mention that she is a licensed minister. In being sensitive for her need to exercise her gift, I would provide teaching moments for her to share the Word of God within the ministry.

As time progressed and the love grew for me, it seemed as though the spirit of competition crept into our house. We would have numerous conversations and she would always point out the negative things.

"They don't listen me!"

"You need to keep your eye on them!"

"Their clothes are too tight!"

"Those girls are in love with you!"

"I can't stand none of them!"

"We need to leave the church!"

There once was a time when one of our young men got locked up in the middle of the night. I received a phone call from the Senior Pastor around 2 a.m. informing me that this young man had been arrested and someone needed to go to the magistrate's office and bail him out.

As I lay in my bed on an early Monday morning trying not to wake up my wife, and knowing that the relationship within the ministry was already delicate, I found myself whispering in the phone to my Pastor, "Don't worry, I'm on my way now."

As I got up, my wife whom I thought was sleeping, admitted to hearing the entire conversation. She was livid.

"Who calls someone this late at night?! Who cares whose son he is?! You're crazy if you get out of this bed! Let him sit there until morning! He will be OK!"

However, knowing the grace that was upon my life, it was imperative that I go and get my spiritual son.

Let's speed this up.

I decided to break a piece of the Youth/Young Adult ministry off and hand it to my spouse. Guess what branch I gave her: the young women.

If this was going to cause my marriage to be easier, then I was willing to provide her with a ministry that she constantly stated she was called to. In doing so, I still maintained my relationship with them and would constantly hear reports that were unfavorable.

These unfavorable reports reached a climax within 30 days when the entire youth department went on a retreat to Williamsburg, Virginia. At this time, my spouse displayed her entire rear end. The situation became so bad over that weekend that the Senior Pastor pulled me into an individual meeting and began to share the challenges and what he had personally heard regarding the adjustment.

We went from growing rapidly to individuals no longer attending teaching times that she was scheduled for. Being unaware of the personal thoughts of the many young adults, I believed everything was moving along fine. Apparently I was oblivious to the monsoon that was hitting the ministry.

I suggested that we have a meeting to discuss these issues. However, after some thought, prayer and a one-on-one conversation with her, I shared that it would be best if she had a meeting with the Senior Pastor and the Youth to discuss what was going on, keeping me out of it.

It was always perceived that I had this relationship within the ministry that I could do no wrong and that they would listen to me before listening to her.

So the meeting happens.

I gave her a clear plan on how to deal with this situation. I encouraged her to hear the youth, listen to the youth, and she would understand the youth. I encouraged her to walk in humility and apologize when appropriate, showing willingness to be accountable for any behavior deemed as inappropriate.

As this meeting takes places, the young women in the ministry attempted to explain that the Senior Pastor and I are the only real father figures that they have in their lives. This is why they listened, honored, and became empowered. As they addressed her behavior as not knowing who it is they would be dealing with due to her frequent attitudes, their personal mistreatment from her, and not knowing which personality was going to show up, conflict ensued.

She did not utilize any of the wisdom I had attempted to share with her. She continued to work against me in ministry, saying the opposite of what I would say, failing to realize her breakthrough was in her ability to see herself within me.

A few weeks later, she decided to leave the ministry, and our family dynamic left with it.

Every man wants a woman who is not only afraid to work a job, but every man wants a woman who is willing to work side by side with them in the ministry. In so many words every man wants a cooperative spouse.

Notes

Notes

5

A Woman Who Isn't Afraid to Ask for What She Wants

In life, due to being rejected, we believe everyone we encounter will reject us when we share our needs and desires which we require to be met. Our mind is a working computer. It recalls our last encounters, memories, and events so that at any random point of time our minds can pull back an idea, thought, feeling, or emotion. Many times when these things happen, we become paralyzed with what has come to our recollection.

Rejection and fear are siblings. They live together. They sleep in the same room together. They dream together. They interpret together. Therefore, a person who is indecisive will struggle in their decision making, requests, and their desires because the twins, fear and rejection, raise their ugly heads at the least opportune time.

Have you ever been trying to fall asleep at night and suddenly, from what seems like out of nowhere, you remember something embarrassing that happened to you ten years ago? You might continue to lay there for the next hour thinking about a rejection that has no effect on your life anymore. The fear that accompanies that rejection is what causes your eyes to remain open.

Imagine believing yourself to be over something that happened long ago, refusing to admit the impact that it continues to play in your life. For example, you thought you had moved on from the childhood molestation you endured, but any time a man attempts to get too close to you, your wall is built so high that he could not even see over it if he tried.

You thought you were over the rejection of your father. You became empowered and an advocate for independence, which secretly robbed you of a gift called interdependence. Interdependence is defined as mutually dependent, or depending on one another. Our refusal to be interdependent will continue to force us into a position where fear and rejection will always be the reigning rulers within one's life. It is imperative that we deal with our issues of feeling as if our need becomes a burden to those who have the ability to do something about it.

An example of this is a young lady on the verge of being evicted from her apartment. Everyone in the family knows she lost her six figure career, however, everyone bases their beliefs off of what she shares. They assume that she received a decent buy-out package when in reality her company offered her a one month's severance package and stated that they would not fight her unemployment claim, knowing that her checking and savings account does not have enough money to keep her afloat. She finds herself in a desperate situation. It's critical. She has a couple of days to come up with this eviction or appear before a judge.

A part of her wants to go to her family, but here comes fear and rejection playing the "Remember the Last Time You Needed Something?" game. She remembers. Those immature days when she would forget to pay her bills, but they could always find her in the club. Those days when she did not know how to prioritize. Those days when they denigrated her. Those days when they showed their disappointment verbally and physically.

They told everybody how irresponsible she was. It went from New York, down to Florida, to Texas, to California, to Colorado Springs, and back to her cell phone. Apparently, she could not do anything right. In the midst of all that talking, her needs were still not met.

Rejection and fear will quickly welcome their cousin pride into the party. Pride says, "You don't need them!"

Fear says, "Be scared to ask them!"

And then there is rejection, completely mismanaging your emotions.

What do you do when you are afraid to ask for what you want? Pride, rejection, and fear say, "Keep your mouth shut!"

Interdependence says, "Although I'm in this season and I very well may not be able to do it by myself, my ability to understand the importance of my need is what is going to force me to put myself out there and push aside that pride, fear, and rejection!"

Although her family did give her grief, they understood that what she was going through was situational and not self-inflicted like before, thus creating a place of healing within the entire family. There had been numerous misconceptions not only about her, but other family members as well. The barriers of miscommunication and false perceptions collided with the wall of reality, unifying the family in ways unimaginable. This created a reconciliation process where everyone joined together to figure out the needs which needed to be met within the family.

According to Ruth 2:7, "And she said, I pray you let me glean and gather after the reapers among the sheaves; so she came, and hath continued even from the morning until now, that she tarried a little in the house" (KJV). Ruth asked for exactly what she wanted. She was precise. She did not go around the corner. She did not beat around the bush. She did not attempt to attain what she wanted illegally. She was specific.

This is a woman who was a foreigner, someone who was not from her current location. She did not know the customs or temperament of the people. In spite of being an outsider, she was confident in what she knew she needed that she refused to allow fear, rejection, and/or pride to cause her to miss out on overflow that was being wasted.

Ruth identified her need and observed how her need could be met. She did not simply show up with a problem, but instead stepped forward with a solution.

Let's apply the needs of the 2017 woman to Ruth. Ruth would not complain that she needs clothes or that she cannot fit into any of her own. She would point to the item that she wants and wait patiently until she receives it. Ruth would not complain about wanting a raise. She would schedule a meeting and prove to her supervisor why she is worthy of one. Ruth would not yell about needing more help around the house, then give no direction as to what she would like done. She would make a list and wait until the tasks are completed.

Ruth refused to be in agreement with fear, rejection, and pride. As a Moabitess, Ruth was accustomed to fear, rejection, and pride because in the land where she came from, those ideals were part of the culture. Even though this was ingrained in her from childhood, Ruth recognized that she could not operate under that system. Due to the new place she was in, that behavior would not be beneficial.

Ungodly fear is classified as the result of estrangement from God. Estrangement is defined as turning away in feeling or affection, even making unfriendly or hostile. 2 Timothy 1:7 states, "For God hath not given us the spirit of fear; but of power, and of love, and of a sound mind" (KJV). The apostle Paul finds himself in a teaching moment with his young protégé, Timothy. Paul recognizes, due to Timothy's young age, that there are times when he (Paul) understands that Timothy could become intimidated. He encourages Timothy to always be mindful of what God has provided him. Paul breaks this thing down and clearly identifies that fear is not something God provides to those He loves and who love Him.

Secondly, Paul advises Timothy of what God does give and identifies power as being one of them. When we operate under the control of fear it renders us powerless.

Thirdly, Paul identifies the attribute of love being another gift God provides. 1 John 4:18 states, "There is no fear in love; but perfect love casteth out fear: because fear hath torment. He that feareth is not made perfect in love" (KJV); when we operate in fear, it diminishes our ability to have an untainted and unconditional love.

Finally, Paul identifies that God provides us with the ability to have a sound mind. Fear takes away our ability to think straight. Fear takes away our ability to have clear thoughts. Fear takes away our ability to remember the truth of God.

Ungodly rejection is classified as the act of denying. Denying is defined as disagreeing with something that is declared and believed to be true, or refusing to recognize or acknowledge. Jesus finds Himself taking a moment to teach his disciples. According to John 15:18, He tells them, "If the world hate you, ye know that it hated me before *it* hated you" (KJV), providing his disciples a realistic understanding that rejection is something that we will all face as a believer of Christ. However, He is admonishing the disciples not to allow the hatred/rejection that they may experience to put them in a place of isolation. Jesus releases the disciples from an isolated state by self-identifying that He understood what it was like to be hated and rejected. He understood rejection so well because he personally experienced rejection from every facet of his life.

According to John 1:11, the apostle John pens these words about Jesus' experience by letting us know He (Jesus) came unto his own, and his own did not receive Him. He came to His own, that is the world. His own received Him not; His own people, the Jewish nation, did not receive him.

Jesus was rejected by His own world in general and by His own people in particular.

To prove this, the prophet Isaiah helps us understand this in Isaiah 53:3 which reads, "He is despised and rejected of men, a man of sorrows and acquainted with grief; and we hid as it were our faces from Him; He was despised, and we esteemed Him not" (KJV). In so many words, the prophet is saying we could not get past what we thought we wanted when it showed up in front of us.

It did not look like we expected it to look.

It did not talk like we expected it to talk.

It did not act like we expected it to act.

It did not even ride into the city on what we were expecting it to ride in on.

Rejection caused the people to miss out on the Savior of the Jews.

Ungodly pride is classified as conceit, self-love, haughtiness, and arrogance. Arrogance is defined as an offensive display of superiority or self-importance, also an overbearing pride. Solomon, a man who inherited the throne from his father King David finds himself in a favorable position with God where whatever he asks, he will receive it. Solomon, a man who saw how his father managed a kingdom, decides to forgo asking for worldly riches. Instead, he asks for wisdom. In his request, God granted him his petition. Solomon finds himself in a position where he utilizes his extreme gift of wisdom to teach the people. He pens these words in Proverbs 11:2a-b:

"When pride cometh, then cometh shame" (KJV). Solomon is letting us know that pride brings something with it. Many times, we think pride only travels with arrogance, conceit, and self-love. However, pride also has a secret, and the secret that comes with pride is shame.

Shame takes us on an emotional rollercoaster, for shame deals directly with the emotion, whereas pride deals with the heart. Both of them have the ability to cripple the believer.

The writer of Psalms 73:6 who pens these words: "Therefore pride compasseth them about as a chain; violence covereth them as a garment" (KJV) wants us to know that many times we are unaware that we are wearing pride around our necks. We do not understand the danger, chaos, confusion, and peril that is visibly seen in the actions, conversations, and behaviors of the believer.

The apostle John unpacks the effects of pride and helps us understand what it does to the believer in 1 John 2:16 where it states, "For all that is in the world, the lust of the flesh and the lust of the eyes, and the pride of life, is not of the Father, but is of the world" (KJV). John, the Revelator, clearly identifies that pride has nothing to do with God, but has everything to do with the world. The dangers of being worldlier than Godly will cause one to operate as an individual who is separated from God. This will cause the individual to accept something that God never intended the believer to have.

Every man wants a woman who is not afraid to ask for what she wants. Every man wants a woman who is clear in her communication. But most importantly, every man wants a woman who is free and who has overcome fear, rejection, and pride.

Notes

Notes

Notes

6

A Woman Who Will Listen and Accept Counsel

What causes us to refrain from accepting counsel from a person? Could it be that we have received so much bad information and advice from an individual that it causes us to no longer trust the words they speak? Could it be that we have previously accepted counsel from an unqualified individual? When I say unqualified, I am talking about the level of experience that person may have in a subject matter. For example, if you need legal advice, you would go to an attorney (I would hope). However, we sometimes tend to go to individuals who have been through a similar situation believing they hold a level of expertise when in all reality, their expertise is based on a limited, trial-by-error working knowledge. Here you are receiving instruction from someone who has not been tested, nor received any educational instruction as to how to make a decision for your life or the lives of those who are in your hands.

This sets us up for numerous failures. This sets us up for broken relationships and we wonder why we are in the same place that we are in.

Listening is not only a skill, but it is an art. The reason listening is considered an art is because it requires a colorful and vivacious dedication to that particular craft. Listening is not something which can be learned in a day, instead it is an art that is honed over time. Listening is a muscle; if that muscle is not exercised it becomes weak. However, if you continue to work out that muscle, your listening skills can expand and grow.

Growing up, my mother used to tell us there are three parts to a conversation. These parts include hearing, listening, and understanding. I know that does not make any sense right now. Let me explain it this way.

My mother used to tell us that when you have a conversation with someone, the first thing we have to do is hear that person. Hearing by definition means *to perceive by the ear*. If we hear the person, we will be able to listen to the person. Listen by definition means *to give attention with the ear* or *to attend closely for the purpose of hearing*. My mother would then go on to tell us that if we could hear her, then we had the ability to listen. Lastly, if we heard the individual, then listened to the individual, then we also had the ability to understand the individual. Understanding by definition means *to grasp the meaning of* or *comprehend the significance, implications, or importance of a subject*.

When we are receiving counsel, if we negate any of these (hearing, listening, and understanding), then we forfeit the ability to understand what is being shared, thus we lose the overall dynamics of what is being shared with us. This has caused many people to lose out on monumental things. People have lost their jobs, their homes, and their relationships all because they were inadequate in the art of listening.

Just take a moment to think about how many conversations that you have had personally where the other party stated that they do not understand what you are trying to say.

"You don't get it."

"You're missing what I am trying to say."

"That's not what I meant."

"You're putting words in my mouth!"

"Out of everything I just said, that's what you got?!"

Many times, we do not get it. Many times, we do not understand it. Could it be that we allowed ourselves to do more talking than hearing? More talking than listening? More talking than understanding?

This is a dangerous place for the person who cannot be told anything. It is dangerous because the said individual acts as though they have attained or ascended to a place they have not even reached. That is a dangerous place to be for it pushes people away from them and causes them to remain in an ignorant state.

When I first saw my wife, it was in the spring of 2006. She was one of the guest speakers for a platform service that our church was having that evening. A friend of mine brought me in the ready-room and introduced me to her. This light-skinned, gray-eyed, gorgeous smile, bright-eyed woman immediately grabbed my attention and I introduced myself. As I walked away, I felt her watching me as I left the room.

She delivered one of the most powerful words from Heaven that I had ever heard that day and I began to become more mesmerized by her.

After service that day, I had an opportunity to converse with her and we exchanged telephone numbers. She was already a designated speaker for our upcoming youth conference. With my being the new Youth and Young Adult Pastor, it was my responsibility to be in contact with her and discuss what role we would like her to play at this event.

A few days passed and I randomly receive a text message from her early in the morning.

She wanted to know if I was awake and had time to talk to her on the phone.

This was about 6 a.m. I responded back stating that yes, I was awake and wanted her to call me.

A few minutes later, she called my phone. She commenced to share that my friend who had introduced us no longer had any time to talk to her while she commuted to work in Northern Virginia because he was in a new relationship. We talked on the phone for over an hour discussing our personal lives as well as our spiritual lives. It appeared that we had so much in common. Both of us raised by our mothers, both of us losing our fathers at a young age, both of us loving the Lord, and both of us desiring marriage.

To me, it seemed like she was the one and I would have to say that it seemed like I was the one for her, too.

As the weeks progressed, we would talk on the phone every day for hours.

The friend who introduced had a birthday coming up and it was expected that both of us be in attendance at which time we were able to be in each other's presence.

From that moment, in my heart, I made the decision that I was going to ask her to be my wife. At this point, I had known her for forty days.

Forty. Days.

We went to both of our pastors independently and discussed our plans with each other. In retrospect, it appears as if our relationship was accelerated due to our relationship being spiritualized.

"Well, you're a preacher and she's a preacher, so this must be God."

"God is in this thing!"

My leaders encouraged me in the relationship, even giving me pointers, tips, and directions.

Soon after, I proposed to her.

But did I mention what my family said?

I was terrified to tell my mother that I was on the verge of getting married, the reason being that a few years earlier

I was dating a pastor's daughter. We were engaged, however one thing led to another and we separated.

Truth be told, I was still in love with this other young lady.

However, I wanted everyone to believe that I was over her. The only way to show everyone who kept talking about her to me that I was over her was by marrying someone that I was never in love with.

I did not tell my in-state family members about my upcoming marriage. I was embarrassed. I knew I was wrong.

My mother told me all the things a mother is supposed to tell me.

"Don't do it."

"She's not the one for you."

"She's not the wife that God has for you."

"You don't know her."

"You haven't given your family the chance to meet her."

"How could you do this?"

Just to think, I was offended by the truth. I stopped communicating with my family. I stopped traveling back and forth up north to see them all because I wanted to live a lie. I refused to accept the counsel of those who loved me the most.

Should I mention that we went through pre-marital counseling? Truth be told, it was a jousting match to see who would land the anointing in their spiritual house.

Who am I talking about?

As bad as this may sound, and the attacks that I may get for this, I am talking about the church.

Our pre-marital counseling consisted of a fighting match over what church we would attend. There was no real counsel, for if there was real counseling, we never would have been married.

One Friday evening, we had prayer at my church and my leader came to me and stated, "God said, it's not too late to back out."

I looked at my leader and told them that I was absolutely sure of what I was doing.

But the only thing I was really sure of was that I was not supposed to get married.

My pride choked out any real answer I could've possibly given and I could only continue to pretend. I did not realize that marrying someone I did not love would cause more damage to my life.

Wedding Day: July 1, 2006.

As the music was playing and my friend who introduced us was singing a song that he wrote for our wedding, you would think seeing my lovely bride walk down the aisle that I would be excited. But as she got closer and closer, I trembled. Not out of fear, but because I knew I was about to go against the will of God for my life.

Here she is, standing next to me, looking as beautiful as ever, reciting her vows, and me reciting mine, knowing that I had been warned, given an exit strategy, and refusing to take it.

Pride's grip was so strong that day that I still said, "I do."

Immediately, the Holy Spirit said, "Now, you know you were not supposed to do that, right?"

I did not know what to do. I just knew that I could not admit to making a mistake.

For a full year, my family barely talked to me. It was not until we found out that we were expecting our first child that things started to change within my extended family.

The consequences of my not listening to the counsel that I was given by the Holy Spirit and by physical people has caused me years of punishment. Even though marriage is honorable in the eyesight of God, disobedience still has a consequence. Although I entered into covenant relationship, God's wrath and discipline was not to be excluded or forgotten. It had to be completed.

Why did it have to be completed?

I needed to be taught the importance of listening and accepting Godly counsel.

Solomon says in Proverbs 11:14, "Where no counsel is, the people fall; but in the multitude of counsellors *there* is safety" (KJV). This is one scripture that I failed to adhere to, and because I failed to accept the counsel that was being provided to me, I moved from a safe place to a place of being subject to the consequences of my decision. These consequences include, but were not limited to: mental abuse, low self-esteem, suicidal ideation, double mindedness, divorce, broken family, child support, back to back court appearances, and even being falsely accused and arrested. My financial livelihood being attacked through the possibility of losing my secret clearance.

It pays to listen.

Would my life be different had I listened?

Absolutely.

But in the midst of not listening, there was a plan. And that plan has led me to get to this day.

According to Ruth 2:8-9, we see Boaz speaking to Ruth stating, "Listen carefully, my daughter. Do not go to glean in another field; furthermore, do not go on from this one, but stay here with my maids. Let your eyes be on the field which they reap, and go after them. Indeed, I have commanded the servants not to touch you. When you are thirsty, go to the water jars and drink from what the servants draw" (KJV).

Ruth had a history and a great level of experience with her husband who was deceased. If we look at this passage of scripture, we see Ruth did not say anything. She listened to the instructions that were given to her. This is important to know here: Boaz told her not to glean in another field, not to leave from where she was, stay with specific people, to keep her eyes on specific people, follow who he asked her to follow, and where to quench her thirst.

If Ruth failed to follow these very simple instructions, she would have been subject to mistreatment, physical abuse, sexual abuse, starvation, dehydration, and she could have been claimed by someone else. Women who worked these fields were typically poor widows who had no living male relatives to support them. If Ruth did not follow Boaz's exact instructions, she could have been subject to anything that was happening on his fields. I would even say that many of us have suffered some level of consequence because we have refused to listen and accept counsel.

Ruth was willing to follow the directions of someone she did not even know. She was willing to allow her internal or innate ability to trust that what was being shared with her was going to be beneficial. Ruth recognized that there was a blessing in listening. She understood that those who listen received a far greater reward and had a greater level of access to abundance and overflow, whereas those who did not listen received just enough to make it through the day or nothing at all.

Ruth decided that overflow was hers, and by understanding that she grasped the art of listening which blessed her and her house tremendously.

A young lady that I know was dating a young man who was not from the United States. He appeared to be everything that she could desire. He had a decent job, money in the bank, he was gentle, attentive, loved the Lord, involved in his local ministry, would pick up the check when they went to dinner, and was the basic epiphany of a gentleman.

But he had secret fear.

His fear was being deported.

He began to pressure this young lady into marriage.

The young lady loved him, but she was not at the place of wanting to be married. She wanted to take more time to develop what it was that they appeared to have.

The young man did not want that. He wanted to be married now to be able to stay in the country.

To make a long story short, she spoke to her most trusted friends and family members who helped her decide what to do. She decided to tell the young man that although she cared for him deeply, she simply was not ready for a marriage.

He did not understand that she was not ending the relationship, but merely stating that she was not ready for marriage. He decided to end the relationship all because she refused to walk into something that she did not want and was not ready for.

Could we imagine the travesty that would have taken place in the lives of these young people getting married for all the wrong reasons?

Every man wants a woman who is willing to listen and accept counsel. Every man wants a woman who is not afraid to receive instructions and directions that will not only save them individually, but then collectively.

Notes

Notes

Thank You

I want to take this time to thank God for changing my life, and allowing me to see through the lens He looks through when He sees me.

I would like to thank my mother Sonya Turane for being my number one supporter, for being there when no one else was, thank you for the many sacrifices you have made to ensure I had every opportunity to succeed in life and thank you for passing down your gift of writing.

To my biological father Clinton Moody I know you're looking upon us from heaven. I hope you're proud of what I have accomplished and proud of whom I'm becoming my life is so much better because you are my dad.

To my beautiful daughter Stephanie aka "Mushi" a.k.a. "Mushface," it is my goal to ensure you become the woman God has created you to be and when He sends your husband you will be prepared to be all that he needs as you are the other side of him. To my one and only son Bryson aka "Bboy," aka "Fatfat" you are an answered prayer, my heart's desire through the grace of God you will be better than me, you will be smarter than me, you will be more successful than me because you are a better me. I will forever love you and your sister in addition to me loving the both of you remember nothing will EVER separate us.

To my siblings Curtis, Clinton, Denzel, Devin, Danyeil and Dana thank you for taking time out of your own lives to listen when I would talk, thank you for encouraging me when I couldn't see my way through the many obstacles that was right in my face.

To the man I affectionately call my dad Superintendent Varrett John Kennedy, I am honored and humbled to have had the opportunity to be raised by you. You have been a beacon of hope, and a steady voice throughout my life and I honor you.

To Apostle Melvin Thompson III thank you for coming to my rescue when I needed it most, thank you embracing me and welcoming me into the ANAN (All Nations Apostolic Network).

To my Pentecostal Holiness family thank you for embracing me, thank you for pushing me, thank you for loving me and thank you for always believing in me. Pastor Marlon and Elder Teesha Harvin you are changing the culture of real Pastoral leadership and I am honored to be a part of such a great work and having the ability to say I love you both dearly.

To the many friends and family who have made my life better I honor you: Apostle Ronald Harvey; Pastor Stefon and Minister Jalissa Spence; Bishop Garry T and Pastor Lisa Rodgers; Pastor Joseph and Minister Cynthia Graham; Minister Jasmin Graham; Minister Demeka McCleave; Rayford and Lady Shema Hooks; Apostle Todd Hudson; Evangelist Teshana Barkley; Apostle Leila Campbell; Ms. Yolonda Evans; Christion Evans and the entire Evans family; Ms. Lena Mae Purifoy aka "Big Auntie;" Ms. Joyce Purifoy; Ms. Lena Purifoy and Lennell; Mrs. Michael and Arnita Shipp; Renee; Michelle we miss you dearly and we know you are smiling as you watch over us every day.

Apostle Shaun Baker the day you ministered at House of God Worship Center the Lord directed you to conduct an altar call and I was hoping not to be called out, and brought to the front but God had to remind me that I needed to get this book to the people. It was the rhema that God revealed to you that pushed and pulled this book out of the spirit and onto these pages. I honor you and the gift that God has blessed you with continue to share what thus saith the Lord with the nation because God is truly speaking through you.

Lastly I want to thank one of my very close friends Mrs. Shemeika Ervin-Mathews. Many people may wonder why I am acknowledging you. And the answer is very simple, when I came to you and shared the vision of the book you immediately helped me critically think it through and assisted in bringing a clear picture to the words I articulated to you.

To my Ambassadors Church of Virginia family OUR future is beyond bright OUR future is glowing so let's take our city, region, state, country and then the world for Christ.

You have been an answered prophecy, you are the epitome of Gods spoken word revealed to not only me but to the entire world and I honor your dedication, patience, trust, faithfulness and push.

Love always,

Raheem Turane

Booking

Please visit www.raheemturane.com to learn more about the ministry of Raheem Turane. Please consider booking Raheem for teaching, preaching or inspirational training events.

Also, prayerfully consider becoming a monthly covenant partner with this ministry so that we can continue to reach the nations with the glorious gospel of Jesus Christ.

Please email your testimonies and or your prayer requests to: raheemturane@gmail.com

Follow Raheem on:
Facebook: @raheem turane ministries
Instagram: @ambassadorraheemturane

Coming Soon

The Woman EVERY Man Wants Vol. 2

The Man EVERY Woman Wants Vol. 1 & 2

Surviving the Unsurvivable

Shade

www.ingramcontent.com/pod-product-compliance
Lightning Source LLC
Chambersburg PA
CBHW020938090426
42736CB00010B/1179